THE CALCULATED RISK

THE MACMILLAN COMPANY
NEW YORK · BOSTON · CHICAGO · DALLAS
ATLANTA · SAN FRANCISCO
MACMILLAN AND CO., LIMITED
LONDON · BOMBAY · CALCUTTA · MADRAS
MELBOURNE
THE MACMILLAN COMPANY
OF CANADA, LIMITED
TORONTO

THE
CALCULATED RISK

Hamilton Fish Armstrong
Editor, "Foreign Affairs"

1947

THE MACMILLAN COMPANY

New York

PRINTED IN THE UNITED STATES OF AMERICA
BY J. J. LITTLE & IVES COMPANY, NEW YORK

CONTENTS

ACKNOWLEDGMENTS

This little book brings together in consecutive form some ideas which I recently presented for discussion in the pages of *The New York Times Magazine* and *Foreign Affairs*. I am most grateful to my associate Byron Dexter for invaluable suggestions and advice throughout, and to Mary H. Stevens, Ann W. Viner and Donald Wasson for their help in checking figures and getting the manuscript ready for the press.

INTRODUCTION

The First World War brought the United States brusquely into its predestined position as a World Power. We became a World Power in every sense save one: we did not acknowledge the fact. We had made a decisive contribution to the victory of democracy and freedom. But we held to the idea that winning a war is like winning a race. We had not learned, and did not want to learn, that in the history of nations nothing is ever finished and settled, that even the supreme test of victory in war writes not just the last sentence in one chapter of responsibilities but also the first in another. There was risk in accepting these new responsibilities; and so we rejected them, in what to shortsighted men seemed a smart decision. What we did not calculate was the risk of refusing them.

The chapter which we as a nation tried so hard to skip began with the organization of the League of Nations. Its last line consisted of two words: Pearl Harbor. What inexorably followed we read, bloody page by bloody page, in suspense and agony. The end came with the hardwon final victories all over the globe.

Once again the last sentence in one chapter became the first in another. This time, however, the American people looked ahead with different eyes. Whereas in 1919 we had felt that success freed us from responsibilities, in 1945 we felt awed by the opportunities which success had brought and sobered by the burdens we knew it laid upon us. In 1919 we had imagined that we ourselves had chosen the part of war, quixotically almost, as palladins of the right; this time we could not escape the fact that it was by the choice of Japan and Germany and Italy that we had had to fight. Then we exulted in the new evidences just given of our national strength and in our security behind our apparently impregnable frontiers. Today, for all the triumphs of our soldiers, sailors and airmen on every continent and sea, the successful leadership of our statesmen in establishing the United Nations, our possession of unrivalled industrial power and the awesome atomic bomb, we have a sense of uncertainty, of dissatisfaction, of work unfinished, of peace still not won, of sadness at the misery and want which surround us.

We are right to be dissatisfied with the condition of the world two years after the victory, but we would be wrong to let our sense of frustration persuade us to change the direction of our policy. So long as our Government keeps its compass set by the same star we must leave it free to show the greatest resourcefulness and vigor of which it is capable. I think we shall. We no longer boast, as Ambassador George Harvey did with such ineffable complacency in 1923: "The national American policy is to have no foreign policy." We have a foreign policy and we believe in it.

The cornerstone of this policy is support for the principles and purposes of the United Nations as set forth in Articles 1 and 2 of the Charter. We ask nothing better than to build on and up from this cornerstone in accordance with the blueprint agreed upon at San Francisco. The fact remains that the attempt of the United Nations to deal with the fundamental problems which cause our greatest anxieties have left many of its adherents wondering whether, all differing ideas as to procedure aside, the members at present do really have sufficiently similar aims to permit them to act effectively so long as the rule of Great Power unanimity prevails. What Mr. Stimson has called the "everlasting No" of one member of the United Nations has paralyzed all its efforts to establish methods to control atomic energy, to provide forces for international police purposes, to limit armaments, to discourage and restrain aggression, and even to concert action for economic recovery.

The urgency of the last-named purpose has already forced us to go outside the framework of the United Nations. As a result of Secretary Marshall's initiative we are about to join in an attempt to restore Western Europe to self-support and self-reliance through the European Recovery Program; and the scope, timing and costs of our part in that Plan are to come into debate in Congress about the time this little book appears in print. The United States adopted this method of direct coöperative action not because we or the other governments concerned wished to ignore the United Nations, but because the organization's economic agencies were still in a formative stage and because the work to be done would not wait on the obstruction of one Power.

Our Government has also been essaying to unfreeze the United Nations by stimulating the General Assembly to exercise various functions of discussion, investigation and report which the Security Council has been prevented from fulfilling, by the veto of the same one Power. If there continues to come from that Power only an "everlasting No" to every attempted preparation for dealing with aggression we may be forced to find a more direct way of reinforcing or supplementing the machinery of the United Nations so that those of its members who wish to carry out their obligations under the Charter may be able to do so effectively.

To help Europe live and to strengthen the United Nations—these are the two main objectives of American foreign policy today. How they can be achieved is the theme of the following pages.

Part I

TO HELP EUROPE LIVE

1.

The visitor today finds Europe abstracted and preoccupied. The Frenchman has always been rather aloof from foreigners, the Englishman complacent toward them, and the German, splitting his back as easily as his personality, ready to lick their boots when he cannot order them around. Such varying symptoms are now transcended by one state which is universal—complete absorption in the problem of how to live. Every minute is dedicated to scrounging enough food, clothing and fuel to carry through the next 24 hours. Little energy is left for noticing what foreign nations think and say or for complicated reasoning and far-sighted planning to please them and suit their requirements, even though they are benefactors and masters of the atom. When you are as worried as Europe is about the bare essentials of existence, you are not much interested in ideas. As for the atom bomb, it is comprehended by most people in Europe even less than by most people in America.

Europeans can satisfy the simplest need today only by efforts out of all proportion, not to its importance, which may literally be vital, but to the former abun-

3

dance which made gratification so cheap and easy. Whatever is not impossible is difficult. Even where the machine of modern civilization has not been destroyed it lacks repairs or fuel or raw materials or accustomed outlets or trained workers or expert management to such an extent that its current production is only a fraction of what its beneficiaries used to take for granted. There is too little of almost everything—too few trains, trams, busses and automobiles to transport people to work on time, let alone to take them on holidays; too little flour to make bread without adulterants, and even so not enough bread to provide energies for hard labor; too little paper for newspapers to report more than a fraction of the world's news; too little seed for planting, too little fertilizer to nourish it and too little equipment to harvest the crop; too few houses to live in, and not enough glass to supply them with window panes; too little leather for shoes, wool for sweaters, gas for cooking, cotton for diapers, sugar for jam, fats for frying, milk for babies, soap for washing.

A striking fact to visitors accustomed to the intense political acuteness of the old Europe is that the passions of this Europe which scrimps, stands in queues, does without, are not closely related to intellectual programs or ideological objectives. Hopes and disappointments are not linked directly to political principles or economic dogmas and do not find expression in firm adherence to Communism or Socialism or capitalism. They are measured in buckets of coal, ounces of bread, packets of cigarettes, and wherever a vote is free it goes where it seems most likely at the moment to increase the supply of these and other life essentials.

In such circumstances the United States is not loved or hated because it is a citadel of political liberty and holds in the main to free enterprise, but according as it seems to be a going concern, measured by its ability and willingness to contribute from its own comfortable fat to strengthen Europe's thin and shivering frame. Nor is the Soviet Union strong because it advertises a certain economic philosophy and promises a proletarian millennium at some future date, or weak because that philosophy is disapproved on theoretical grounds and because the doorstep to that millennium is dictatorship. It, too, is judged by whether or not it seems a going concern, measured by its relative contributions to the improvement of the European economy and the ability of its agents, the heads of the various national Communist parties and the Communist chiefs of the labor unions, to appear as the strongest protagonists of the masses and to gain them food and wage advantages.

The first tendency after the war was to judge the United States rather severely and to make allowances for Soviet Russia. More was expected of us than of Russia because our wartime prodigies of production made us seem capable of anything we would put our minds to, and because our territories were not laid waste and Russia's were. This handicap, however, has gradually been modified, mainly because Soviet Russia's claims are so much more sweeping than ours. We have not asserted that our doctrines are infallible, that our political system does not leave room for improvement, that our economy is not subject to ups and downs. We have not entrusted to our government the responsibility of regimenting all our thoughts and planning all our actions. We doubt that human capacities include the wit to foresee so accurately the tempers of men or the limitations that Providence and the weather may set on their performance.

Marxist Russia has claimed this infallibility and invited these responsibilities. She says categorically that our economic organization and social institutions are putrid and prophesies that capitalism must soon topple into its grave. The dogma that free enterprise is doomed to be succeeded by collectivism is as unyielding as another of the dogmas thought up by Karl Marx 80 years ago (and since consistently controverted by the history of the United States), namely, that capitalism = imperialism = war. Does Marxist Russia maintain it so unblinkingly in order to divert attention from the fact that her totalitarian economy does not "produce the goods"—consumer goods, heavy equipment or food—to satisfy the needs of her own people, let alone a sufficient surplus to restore and revivify Europe? This might count for much or little if ideologies were the chief currency in Europe today. But if it is a fact that the present currency for winning esteem is mainly material, the advantage lies with us to the extent we choose to exercise it.

The statement that Europe is preoccupied with material problems is a generalization and so has exceptions. Some of the exceptions are more apparent than real. Thus, numbers of persons register with the Communist Party in order to deserve favorable treatment if it should come to power (knowing they will not suffer if, on the other hand, democracy should win); but such invertebrate opportunism can hardly be rated as a form of political consciousness. Again, D.P.s, ex-prisoners of war and even ex-partisans form a reservoir of unemployed which organizers of illegal movements can tap in enlisting undercover agents and front fighters; some of these may still be possessed of political zeal, but more are simply hungry for adventure with pay. Definitely in the class of the politically conscious, of course, are the intellectuals and men of affairs who struggle to overcome the effects of their wartime isolation, revive the popular faith in democratic institutions and adapt liberal economic principles to Europe's present abnormal necessities. Their declared enemies are similarly busy—the cautiously reëmerging Fascist who hates democracy as much as he hates Communism, and the able and omnipresent spokesman for Communism whose every word and act follow Moscow's telegraphic instructions. However, these two groups, extreme right and extreme left (still so considered, at any rate, perhaps erroneously), are professionals. In between lies the great mass of what some Americans call, with a self-conscious avoidance of condescension that would turn the stomach of a natural democrat like Jefferson, "the common man." These are strictly amateur, shifting from party to party by whim and instinct based on the latest supply of meat in the markets, the latest rumor in the bread queues, the latest blackmarket price of tobacco.

European leaders whose views are not colored by some totalitarian philosophy are subject to the same myopia as the man in the street, even though the objects that engage their attention are of national dimensions instead of "family size." To the extent that the average man notices international events at all he is apt to wonder whether they will put more potatoes in the soup and less straw in the cigarettes. Similarly, the statesman asks: Will they bring more bushels of wheat across the Atlantic? Will they deliver more tons of coal from the Ruhr? For the specter of an empty national breadbasket, an empty national coalbin, an empty national treasury, obsesses a national leader in just the same way that hunger and an empty pocketbook make an individual incapable of even pretending to take an interest in questions of high policy.

2.

The whole Continent west of the iron curtain thus remains debatable ground for ideas and ideologies. The old ideas of the French Revolution have not regained possession of its heart and mind and the new propositions of Lenin and Stalin have not established themselves in their stead. That debate is only just beginning. You cannot eat either "Das Kapital" or the Declaration of the Rights of Man. When Europe has money that is worth working for, and something to buy with it, she will again develop the intellectual and spiritual energies to understand and debate and decide. Until then she will at best hang fire, as it were, not opting definitely for our aims in life, but on the other hand not turning from them decisively; at the worst, the accumulations of uncertainty and misery will throw her over into civil strife and chaos.

All of Europe's weaknesses and contradictions were laid bare in the reaction to President Truman's proposal in April 1947 that the United States help consolidate the internal situations in Greece and Turkey as a means of enabling the governments of those countries to resist threatened encroachments from abroad. The hopes of European democratic leaders leapt up at seeing the United States preparing to stay in Europe and contribute to the stabilization of nations threatened with social disintegration. At the same time, they could not help being worried at the intimation that everyone must now choose sides in an ideological battle, the more so as our decision not to act through the United Nations was taken at first to mean that we thought the time for negotiating specific problems in the world forum was over.[1]

In adopting this cautious view these Europeans were not craven; there was a plausible enough reason why they should want to postpone an ideological show-down as long as possible. All through Europe the Communist parties after the war had attracted millions of voters who wished merely to protest against every-thing as it was. There were, as indicated above, ex-ceptions—the fearful who wanted to hedge against the risks of a possible Communist victory, and the workless and rootless (the *Geächteten* of Ernst von Salomon's novel of that name in the twenties) who found adventure with pay as seditionists or guerrillas. But many of the millions who had simply registered protest votes for Communist candidates, and even some of the others, could logically be expected to drift back to Socialist or various liberal parties whenever the economic situation improved and the social structure became more stable; for when that happened they would be free from the compulsion to think about

[1] On this point, at Senator Vandenberg's suggestion, the State Depart-ment and Congress promptly found means to set the record right.

ways of existence instead of about ways of life. Various
leaders of tested devotion to democracy therefore hoped
sincerely that the United States would not press for
a showdown until economic recovery was on the way;
and in the spring of 1947 it patently was not.

From the American view there were strong answers
to this line of argument. The President and Secretary
of State have the responsibility of planning the defense
of our national interests all over the world. Some
American writers advise a cautious policy restricted
to the defense of our interests in spheres where our
power is preponderant and immediately available. That
policy has the attraction of being comparatively easy
to execute; but it is not enough. Diplomacy's true and
harder task is to defend the whole national interest
wherever it is in jeopardy, outside as well as within
the area of instant national power. Even former isola-
tionists and advocates of limited risks have found it
increasingly difficult to devise convincing frontiers for
what they used to call "the American region." Still
less, of course, are the President and Secretary of State
able to rely on a mere probability that events far afield
will leave the long-term interests of the United States
untouched.

President Truman's appeal to the Congress in April
1947 for funds to strengthen the defensive forces of
Greece and Turkey against the expansive forces of
the Balkan satellites of Soviet Russia does not seem

to have been intended to force the pace in Europe as a whole or induce European nations to "choose sides." He cannot have been oblivious to the tragic dilemma of European statesmen standing directly beneath the half-lowered iron curtain and liable to be crushed at any moment beneath it, nor would he be unsympathetic towards some of the others who though not quite so precariously placed nevertheless endure daily invectives and threats from the Communist minorities in their own parliaments. He seems simply to have decided that if a showdown refused to wait until the middle-of-the-roaders felt themselves ready for it, he would have to accept the Soviet challenge, wherever it might be presented, and act as effectively as possible to protect the world-wide American interest.

The suggestion put forward by Secretary Marshall on June 5 was in one sense a generalization of the Truman Doctrine. But in a wider sense it was an effort to transform what had been an essentially negative policy of restraining the Soviet Russian flood at specific weak points into a positive policy of restoring the European fabric as a whole to such a state of well-being that it would be impervious to Communist infiltration and so make military and political measures superfluous. As Secretary Marshall was careful to point out: "Our policy is directed not against any country or doctrine but against hunger, desperation and chaos."

In concrete terms, Secretary Marshall's suggestion was that the European nations agree on a long-range program of mutual self-help, and that the United States give them assistance in money and goods to put it into effect and carry it to success. The proposal was seized on with enthusiasm and relief by statesmen throughout Europe, including—until peremptory orders to the contrary went out from Moscow—the leaders of at least two countries in the Soviet zone. Probably Secretary Marshall himself was surprised by the warmth of this welcome; certainly some of the European leaders whose feelings about the Truman Doctrine had been to say the least mixed must have been amazed to find themselves able to endorse this adaptation and expansion of it so warmly. The fact is that American observers in Europe who had advised a bold economic initiative, even at the cost of a political showdown, and European statesmen who had wished to delay a political showdown until after economic recovery had actually begun, were both in a sense justified. The mere portent of firm and effective economic action became a strong catalytic agent in European politics; and when evidence accumulated that the American public and Congress inclined to make Secretary Marshall's objectives their own, the European scene underwent a transformation.

The first sign came from the European Socialists. Right-wing members of Socialist parties who had hesitated to oppose the Communist tactic of the "common front" began going out to battle with their fellow-traveller colleagues. Then came successive indications of a new political temper in several countries, notably France, Norway, Denmark and Britain. The falling off of the Labor vote in the British municipal elections may have come largely from disgust with austerity and disillusionment with the results of nationalization. But in the other elections international issues bulked large, and they all revealed a pronounced swing to the center and right. In addition, in Italy and France, where Communist blackmail had been most open, there was a tendency for moderate groups which had been fighting each other to coalesce against the common enemy. On a frankly anti-Communist platform, de Gaulle gathered in about 40 percent of the French vote from various established parties, even carrying the big industrial cities. And in Italy, Guglielmo Giannini, the neo-Fascist head of the "Common Man Front," who had been flirting with the Communists in an effort to bring down the de Gasperi Government and defeat the Marshall Plan, found himself deserted by the half of his 34 deputies who favored constitutional political methods and orderly economic recovery.

The simple fact that the governments of 16 nations had been able to agree on their joint economic and financial needs over a four-year reconstruction period, and that the Truman Administration was prepared to ask Congress to appropriate funds to carry the American share of the program into effect, was sufficient to allow the more than 200 million inhabitants of those nations to begin hoping again. And the mere advent of hope changed votes and political programs.

3.

We want to help the people of Europe to escape, in our interest and theirs, from the isolation of misery, confusion and apprehension in which they have been living. We want to carry them word that we still care about them as we did when we landed on the Channel beaches. We want them to know that we hold hard to the same course we set when we put our signature to the Charter of the United Nations. We want them to understand that our system of democratic government and private enterprise is living and growing, adapting itself to the needs of the present as it did to those of the past. We want them to remain part of the civilization of which they were so largely the originator and so long the center. We want them, in this sense, to be with us.

If we can achieve the first purpose, the others will probably follow. Without the first we can achieve none. In our pocketbooks and storehouses and machine-shops and mines we have at hand the means for that first success; in the Marshall Plan, as elaborated

in the 16-nation Report and the European Recovery
Program, we have the method.

In Eastern Europe we had to watch helplessly while,
one after another, strongly individualistic nationali-
ties, representatives of old civilizations, were toppled
over by Soviet bayonets into the anonymous Soviet Sea.
Communist doctrine did not prove itself superior to
democratic doctrine in the minds of most Poles or
Hungarians or Serbs. Nevertheless, the application of
Soviet force to them and many others similarly situated was, and for the time being remains, decisive.

In Western Europe, however, Soviet Russia has
found herself operating under very different conditions from those prevailing in countries which were
occupied by her troops, or, having passed through that
ordeal, have come out full-fledged Soviet satellites,
ready for amalgamation into an East European Fed-
eration of Soviet Republics. We too find ourselves dif-
ferently situated there. The governments of Western
Europe do not at present contain Communist members and do not operate across the street from a Soviet
Kommandatura and alongside an NKVD headquar-
ters. In the absence of these convenient stimuli, the
"revolutionary situation" which in the Marxian bible
precedes the act of revolution requires a good deal
more arranging; and by the same token we have very
different opportunities for preventing it from being
arranged.

When these lines appear in print Congress will have

begun to debate the 16-nation Report,[2] the long-range
European Recovery Program based upon it, and the
Administration's request for funds to supply stop-gap
relief to France and Italy until the long-range program can be studied, digested, modified if necessary,
and, hopefully, approved. These plans will not be discussed here in their technical aspects. What is much
more important, and will be discussed, is the spirit and
manner in which we approach them.

First of all, we cannot afford to be either parsi-
monious or timid. If our outlay in money and effort
is not to be wasted it must be very large and must
continue for a long time. Europe has spent ten out
of the last thirty-three years in war, and many of her
best energies in the years of so-called peace went into
restoring damage already done and in preparing to do
greater damage the next time. This is not said in cen-
sure; the United States was in those wars too. The
point is that a quarter-century of war and armistice
has wrecked the European machine, and that the cost,
effort and time necessary to repair, refuel, restaff and
get it going again will be enormous.

[2] Committee of European Economic Co-operation, vol. 1, General Report; vol. 11, Technical Reports. (Department of State Publications 2930
and 2952. U.S. Government Printing Office, Washington, D.C., 30 cents
and $1.00.) The basic documents on the American side are the reports
of the Krug, Nourse and Harriman committees, appointed by President
Truman to examine into our natural resources, the impact of our foreign
aid program on our own economy, and, in the light of these findings,
the safe and wise limits of our assistance. (For full summaries of these
three reports see *The New York Times* for October 19, November 2 and
November 9, 1947.)

First emphasis should not in my opinion be put where ex-President Hoover was inclined to put it. Mr. Hoover asked whether we can afford to supply the resources that Europe must have to be enabled to begin releasing her own forces of production, applying again her old skills, creating currencies which encourage work and gradually resuming her old place in world trade. To my mind, the primary question is not how great an effort we can afford, but what effort is necessary?

This is not fantastic or unrealistic or spendthrift. It is the way Americans are accustomed to act. It is the way we acted in the war. We did not ask: "Can we afford to defend America?" We paid taxes, increased the national debt and bought bonds for a combined total of something like 335 billion dollars to keep the Nazis and Japanese from defeating us and subjecting us and the rest of the world to dictatorship, exploitation and suffocation. If the fighting war had continued another six months, as it very well might, we would not only have had to sacrifice thousands of lives more to win through to victory, but would have paid out another twenty-five or thirty billion dollars without stopping to count it. Are we prepared today to think in some such terms as that in order to make the victory stick? Lives are not being asked. But dollars in a very great amount are asked, to validate the sacrifice of lives already spent to prevent a totalitarian police state from seizing the world by force, and on the chance that if another is being tempted to try the same gamble it may thus be dissuaded, without our sacrifice of more lives and immeasurably greater numbers of dollars.

The real unrealists, I can't help thinking, are those who cast up our national account solely in material terms. Certainly the effect on our own living costs and wages of a great increase in our shipments abroad, without a corresponding increase in our imports, is an essential item in our national calculations. But other items which are less tangible are not less important. When we are considering what our effort in Europe must and can be, we should calculate not only the risks of making such an effort but also the risks of not making it. For this purpose we must estimate the likely effect on our economy, basic social structure and national security of a complete breakdown of Europe into chaos and strife, and weigh these against the likely risks and hardships of acting beyond what may seem the limits of our strength.

Secondly, we cannot afford to assume the haughty role of the grand almoner who is infallible about everything. We may even have to adopt a self-denying ordinance in one of the fields of our fondest beliefs. The Communists have calculated that supposing we did join in a European recovery program we nevertheless would hedge our contribution about with so many self-righteous provisos and entangle the beneficiary countries in so many arbitrary commitments that what we thought of as an act of unprecedented generosity could be painted by the Kremlin's propagandists as an insidious snare to exploit Europe, dominate its economic future and tie its currencies irretrievably to the imperial dollar. Their speeches are already being written, and by courier and cable are being sent, like the tidings of Lars Porsena of Clusium, east and west and south and north. To keep from tumbling into this pitfall we shall have to avoid seeming to make our program of help contingent on Europe's repudiation and avoidance of many things that are not in the book of American capitalism (though not so strictly outside American practice in times of crisis as those who write the books sometimes indicate). Government planning, government controls, nationalization, can all be attacked as "Marxist." It will not be wise for us to make that sort of attack indiscriminately. We can argue properly and perhaps effectively that no program should be adopted with our help simply *because* it is Marxist, and we can point out the dangers of permanently saddling a national budget with the functions and functionaries created to handle a temporary job of, say, rationing or rent control. But we move into uncertain territory if we demand that a particular emergency policy shall be omitted because it has Marxist sanction; and Congressmen with two or three relatives on the government payroll should not be too self-righteous about swollen bureaucracies in indigent foreign countries. We are not trying to impose capitalism, precisely as we understand it at this moment, on Europe. If we attempted that we should fail. What we want to achieve is that as many nations as possible shall have an opportunity to decide, by democratic means and at a time in the future when they have alternative choices before them, what sort of economy they want.

Closely connected with the above, we should consider how to make the face we show in Europe represent more closely the rugged visage of the United States, how to make our voice there ring out with more of our native confidence, and how to reveal that the warm heart which the world readily grants we possess is matched by a clear head and a spirit that John Gunther has called American "spring-mindedness." This is a task more for the State Department than for Congress; though if the State Department is to perform it adequately Congress must reverse the obsession of some of its members with short-term economy and back up the billions it is preparing to spend on European reconstruction with an adequate appropriation for information and education. As the people of Europe begin to find time to think and plan for the future, it is essential that they have at hand a proper measure for judging the propaganda of the Communists to the effect that the United States represents everything decadent in modern life.

Of course the first step in giving the right impression is that we shall in fact be what we claim to be.

We know we are far from perfect; but we would like to be credited with being at least as good as we are. Our detractors commonly say that because we believe in the same fundamental freedoms we struggled to establish in the past we have stopped short in our development. It is not enough for us to reply that our principles of representative government and our system of free enterprise have given us the highest standard of living and the closest approximation to social justice and freedom of opportunity that the world has ever seen. We must in addition show that our institutions are capable of extension and improvement to meet modern needs and desires, and that we are constantly busy extending and improving them—as, to cite just one reform and one development, by the SEC and the TVA. Our diplomatic representatives should visit factories at least as often as they dedicate monuments, should get to know labor leaders and intellectuals more intimately, and should speak more about our free schools and universities, our research institutions and hospitals, our minimum wage for workers, our old age and sickness insurance, our restrictions on monopolies and cartels. These and many other things which need to be known, but which we can hope to make known only slowly, should not be advertised in a tone of bumptiousness or superiority, but merely as matters of fact. The tone makes the music. And in talking about yourself it is especially hard to hit the right note in the long gamut between shrillness and inaudibility.

But to return to the current debate. It will not be sufficient for Congress merely to have the wisdom and ingenuity to avoid handing Communist propagandists the arguments they count on being able to use to tarnish and discredit the European Recovery Program. Congress should aim consciously by every means to give its billions the strongest possible impact on European opinion. The Communists say not merely that we aim to tie Europe to the chariot of the imperial dollar, but also that we are flighty as a people and unreliable as a government. Just as Congress can disarm the first libel by avoiding the assumption of economic omniscience, so it can forestall the second by making available whatever sum it decides Europe needs for the full period it decides Europe needs it. Congress has the duty to study the requests of the 16 nations and the Administration's recommendations based upon them with care and at length; but when it finally makes up its mind to act it should bring itself to do so on the whole program of reconstruction rather than on just a section of it. There will be a strong temptation to appropriate funds for only the first year, leaving other sessions of Congress to appropriate the other three installments. For one thing, each annual appropriation could in that case be said to be covered out of the expected annual budgetary surplus. Further, this method would appear to make it easier to hold the

European recipients to the fulfillment of their part of the bargain as regards production targets, financial reforms and the reduction of trade barriers. Actually, of course, it makes no real difference in our national pocket whether a budget surplus is used to finance the European aid program or to retire other government obligations. As for control, a government corporation, entrusted with funds for the full four-year period, could require quarterly reports from the receiving countries and make allocations available to them on a quarterly basis; and this form of control over disbursements would be more effective than any which Congress could exercise through annual appropriations. Nor need this procedure deprive Congress of any prerogatives. Congress could insist on sharing in the choice of the director and members of the nonpartisan board appointed to administer the corporation; it could draw up detailed instructions for their guidance; and it could set up a special joint committee like that created under the Atomic Energy Act, to keep in close touch with the new agency's operations.

The greatest boon, of course, would be that Congress would not have to go through the same debate every year for four years, raising both questions of principle and procedure afresh and arguing them out as though they had not already been thoroughly discussed. One fight now for the full sum might be somewhat harder than a fight for just the first instalment, but the greater effort required to win it would almost certainly be less than the total of four annual efforts. And the saving in oratory would be immense. Most important of all, prompt adoption of the complete program would be the strongest possible earnest of our determination to carry the Marshall Plan through to complete success; the impact on European public opinion would be the maximum, and it would come now, when it is needed most.

Incidentally, there is no reason either of morals or finance why the full sum of money needed to carry the Marshall Plan to completion should all come out of current account. We properly speak of this program as designed to help guard the interests and lives of our children. There is no reason why one part of it should not be financed by Government bonds rather than by appropriations voted by a reluctant Congress and covered out of current taxes. The goods, however, do have to come out of current account. We might decide to leave our children to pay some of the money costs, but not the costs in labor and materials. They have to be contributed now. For this purpose we must keep our factories, mines, farms and railroads operating at capacity. Otherwise we shall have nothing to share.

To operate a foreign reconstruction program effectively the President requires certain extraordinary powers. He must be able to separate our total production of certain commodities into the part to be retained for domestic consumption and the part, small by comparison, which would be set aside for foreign reconstruction; and he must be able to make sure that the latter actually reaches the countries designated in the over-all plan. For some of the powers needed to do this he has asked already; for others he presumably will ask as he encounters specific difficulties in administering fairly an enterprise with ramifications throughout our domestic life as well as affecting the lives of over 200 million people in 16 diverse foreign countries. The success of the program will be settled in large part by what farmers and processors and manufacturers do at earlier stages, long before specific items of food appear on hotel menus or in grocers' and butchers' shops. A detailed and mandatory system of allocations and controls must be in operation to protect the American householder against a continuing spiral of shortages and rising prices. Only the Government has the information on which to base decisions in areas of complicated action (for example, to prevent the diversion of abnormal quantities of wheat from human to animal consumption); and only the Government has the power to subordinate special interests to the common interest.

What can we—must we—do as individuals to help? Secretary Marshall has said that "the attitude of Americans toward food can make or break our efforts to achieve peace and security throughout the world," and that as a result "our foreign policy has entered the American home and taken a seat at the family table."

How are we responding individually to this challenge?
How are we treating this problem guest?

Badly, because we have been asked too little. We
have been asked by President Truman to waste less
and eat less, and to this end he has suggested various
voluntary methods of limiting the national use of certain key commodities. This procedure is not effective
and it is not democratic. That it is not effective our
eyes give daily evidence wherever we happen to live,
and newspaper reports and public opinion polls confirm the fact for the country as a whole. It is not democratic, because the sacrifices which the well-informed
and conscientious make for the benefit of the needy
abroad can be partly nullified by the self-indulgence of
the badly-informed and conscienceless at home. Only
the Government can insist that available supplies really
are shared equally.

I referred earlier to Europe's need for an early boost
in morale. Evidently we need one, too. Adoption of an
effective and democratic program of saving and sharing would supply it more quickly than anything else.
If anyone objects that we already have plenty of morale, then I would turn my argument around and say
that we might export a measure of it to Europe, paid
for at this end by a certain number of equally-shared
self-deprivations.

Actually, they need not be very onerous. Not even
in the midst of the war did we ever have to "do without" as most people in Britain and in many countries

on the Continent are doing today. Of course the restrictions would have to be explained, with the same
urgency and conviction that the need for wartime
restrictions and the purchase of war bonds was explained. This produces another argument in favor
of real rationing: in order to justify it, Administration
officials would have to throw themselves into the job
of "selling" the European Recovery Program on a
scale and with an intensity that so far seems not to
have occurred to anyone in Washington.

The campaign of enlightenment might tell us, for
example, that hotels in New York throw away more
meat in scraps in a day than many good-sized cities in
Europe have received that day to supply their whole
populations. We have for some time had plenty of
sugar for our coffee and tea (and coffee and tea to
put it in). The Government ended the rationing of
sugar a few months ago because its plea to the International Emergency Food Council had resulted in an
increased allocation of sugar, which gave us 7,150,000
tons a year, compared to the 6,700,000 tons we con-
sumed before the war. Would the American people
have insisted on this increased allocation if they had
known that millions of Europeans would meantime
continue sugarless? We have coal and gas and oil to
light our houses and offices and to keep them much
too warm in winter for our own good. Would we not
turn off some electric signs again and cut down the
temperature of our rooms by two or three degrees if

we were told that it would save some Europeans from freezing to death this winter? I do not say that to-bacco is an essential, though some think it so. Enough butts of cigarettes that smokers have not taken the trouble to more than half consume lie every evening in the gutters around Fifth Avenue and Forty-second Street to break the black market in Vienna or Milan if an equivalent in cigarettes were sent there for dis-tribution through legal channels.

If in these circumstances our morale is not sufficient to support certain specific measures of compulsory ra-tioning, so that our Government may be able to ex-port a little of our morale to Europe in the form of food and fuel, then we simply are spoiled and need to be told so. The person to tell us is the President of the United States. He should tell us in specific terms, as part of his comprehensive plan for securing the money and supplies to rehabilitate Europe, what we are doing that we ought not to be doing, and what we are not doing that we ought to be doing. When this subject was raised a few months ago it was said that any form of rationing in peacetime was "unthink-able"; but it has proved ineffective, and with it prices have continued to rise. In any case, this is not peace-time. That is the first home truth which the President might tell us on behalf of a program including any-thing as unpalatable as compulsory rationing. And if the President decided to support such a program, and gave his reasons patiently, in the terms of conscience and patriotic duty which would indeed be justified, it might turn out to be less lethal politically than his political advisers would predict. It might even label him with such a shining title to statesmanship that the little men who opposed it would be the only sufferers.

4.

It will be asked what reason there is to suppose that Soviet Russia will delay in forcing a general showdown with us if time now is really working in our favor in Europe. Indeed, it may be argued that her leaders have already moved in the direction of a showdown—by refusing to coöperate in the Marshall Plan and then by vowing to defeat its objects, by vetoing the proposal of the Security Council majority to establish a watch over the inflammable Greek frontier, by boycotting a commission which the General Assembly then set up for that purpose, and by creating the Belgrade "Cominform" to coördinate the propaganda offensive of revolutionary Communism. Of course, we do not know the reasoning back of these moves. The decision to hold aloof from the Marshall Plan may have been taken in the calculation (or, as it turned out, the miscalculation) that the task of European reconstruction would seem to us too great to be attempted without Soviet help, and hence that instead of redoubling our efforts we would withdraw. If such Soviet expectations of victory through a default on our part existed they soon died, and were succeeded by a declaration of economic warfare. General Zhdanov, who had represented the Politburo at the meeting in Poland when the Cominform was organized, announced as an immediate Soviet objective "to see that the Marshall Plan is not realized." Similarly, the splurge of vetos in the Security Council may have aimed merely to probe how far Soviet manoeuvres could extend before they encountered a hard core of resistance. If so, Mr. Vishinsky's tirades after Secretary Marshall's address in the General Assembly perhaps revealed an angry realization that the resistance point was closer than the Kremlin's diplomatic agents abroad had ever mustered courage to tell it.

Other factors support the interpretation that Soviet Russia is conscious of playing from weakness rather than strength and so may still be supposed to be engaged in propaganda manoeuvres rather than a program of planned provocation.

One is her own probable weakness. Some twelve million Russians have been killed, the most productive areas of Soviet territory have been devastated, and much of the Soviet industrial plant and transport system is in disrepair. The Soviet Government's inability to supply its own population with everyday necessities and conveniences is so great that anywhere else the Communists would present it as a reason for a

revolution. Most observers report that the Russian people want war no more than do Americans. This means
very little; in a dictatorship the lives of millions—let
alone their wishes—are of negligible account when the
ruling caste is considering major decisions of policy.
Much more important is the apparent fact that the
country's physical condition today is not such as to encourage Marshal Stalin and the Politburo to make
war, even on the supposition (for which there of course
is no proof) that they would like to do so. Beyond all
this is the fact of the atom bomb. The Kremlin real-
izes we will never use it unless we are directly menaced
or attacked. Our possession of it thus does not
strengthen our diplomatic hand, and indeed weakens it
by laying us open to Communist villification for trying
to coerce the world through the threat of atomic
destruction. Nevertheless, the Kremlin must have a
thoroughly realistic knowledge of the value of the
bomb to us in the event of hostilities. Soviet foreign
policy thus can be exceedingly strong up to a certain
point; but it has a weak base.

A second factor is Soviet Russia's decreased prestige
in areas where she has been on exhibition since the
end of the war. The spectacle of Russia's heroic defense of her homeland and successful repulse of the
invader, which so aroused the world's enthusiasm, was
followed by an irruption of Soviet troops into eastern
and central Europe. These troops have not turned out
to be envoys of Soviet good will or even advertisements

of Russian might. They came as liberators but stayed as locusts. They are badly dressed, crudely fed, and their equipment is startlingly inferior to that of the other Allied troops of occupation. They are now kept out of sight as much as possible. Their avid appropriation of personal belongings and household gear was actually less damaging to Soviet prestige than the way Soviet agents dismantled village mills, local power plants and small bridges, and shipped the parts off to Russia, along with antique river craft, trolley-cars of Toonerville design and the rails they had run on. The rather unfair feeling—unfair in view of the Nazi devastation in Russia—was that if the Soviet colossus needed such primitive equipment so desperately its collectivized economy had not made all the strides advertised at the end of successive five year plans.

Beyond all this, of course, the populations of eastern and central Europe, especially those that recall fierce struggles for freedom and have a memory of self-government, resent the Soviet pressure which has put them under minority Communist parties. The fact is that wherever Russian Communism has been felt on a people's own skin—whether in the Soviet zones of government in Germany and Austria, or in a country with an indigenous Communist dictatorship like Jugoslavia—a violent irritation has been set up, with a resulting tendency toward immunity. Today there is no impartial observer who estimates the true believers in Communism in any state outside the frontiers of

Soviet Russia at more than one-quarter or one-third
of the population, and sober estimates for most of the
countries of Eastern Europe run much lower. In the
case of Poland, for example, the Communist minority
(excluding Soviet troops and officials) is not put at
higher than 5 or 10 percent, and for Rumania an even
smaller figure is usually given. Of course, any sign of
hostility in a country under Soviet occupation or
domination is dealt with summarily; the head that
shows above the level of its subject fellows is simply
knocked off. And in the course of several generations,
national consciousness and the remembrance of freedom may be extirpated. But that has never been ac-
complished in the past by Teutonic knights or Turk-
ish pashas or Austro-Hungarian bureaucrats or Nazi
butchers. And certainly for the present Soviet Russia
must reckon on finding that her rule has made fewer
friends for Communism proportionately in, say, Rumania or Bulgaria than Franco's rule has made for
Communism in Spain. This essential weakness of dictatorships can be revealed only when some great up-
heaval releases native forces at the same time that a
realignment of world forces is in progress; but this,
again, might be another reason why Soviet Russia
would be cautious today about loosing a world cata-
clysm.

Account should be taken, thirdly, of the probability
that in some of the European countries the Communist
parties are not as strong as they have seemed. Local

Communist leaders have often been dismayed by the policies which Moscow imposed upon them. In France, for example, they realized that support of revolution in Indo-China and Madagascar, useful as it might be in Soviet schemes for the disintegration of empires, did not sit well with the French public. Similarly, Italian Communists were greatly discomfited by the orders they received from Moscow all through the debate over Trieste. True, the trade unions in France, Italy and other continental nations have come into the control of Communist Party members; and at their simple order labor can completely cripple the national life. But so far the order is withheld.

In stressing these factors we may be falling into the common error of underestimating the blind dogmatism and ruthless unconcern for human life which characterize the modern "scientific" dictators. Nor must we forget that when an unforeseen success of their adversaries throws them onto the defensive, they are apt to react fanatically and regardless of cost, as in their rejection of the Marshall Plan. The Cominform signalized the open abandonment by Communist parties in Europe of coöperation with left-wing non-Communist parties. The manifesto establishing it stigmatized the leading Socialists of Europe as traitors— Léon Blum, Paul Ramadier, Clement Attlee, Ernest Bevin, Karl Renner, Kurt Schumacher, Giuseppe Saragat. And the terms of its appeal for coördinated revolutionary efforts was an admission that the political

contest could no longer be waged under cover of pre-
tended adherence to legality and democracy.

The Soviet tacticians must nevertheless be reminded
by the Soviet military of the risks of bringing the political conflict to a head in any of the major west
European countries through a prolonged general
strike, for this would be liable to produce a civil war
and that in turn could easily become a general war.
Marshal Stalin and the other members of the Politburo, General Zhdanov included, must know that
not only would we increase our economic and financial
support for legal régimes endangered by civil war, but
that we also would promptly supply them with the
arms that international law entitles them to purchase
from us. At the start of the Spanish civil war we refused to let the Spanish Republican Government, le-
gally elected and constitutionally operating by majority
will, buy arms to defend itself against a Fascist revolution. That break with international custom and our
own tradition cost us dear, and we would not be apt
to repeat it. In these circumstances, even a highly op-
timistic or thoroughly frightened Soviet diplomat
would hesitate to put his name to a prediction that the
United States would stand by and watch Italy and
France torn by civil war without initiating in return
a series of formidable defensive actions.

The fanaticism of at least some Communists forbids
us, evidently, to disregard entirely the possibility that
the Soviet Government may not be able to make a

correct calculation of its own interest. Nor is such fanaticism its only handicap in judging the temper of other nations. Thirty years of uninterrupted Communist self-indoctrination have dulled Russian wits, as the deterioration of official Soviet propaganda from that conducted by able dialecticians like Bukharin and Radek to the empty name-calling of Vishinsky reveals. Also, since the only protection for even the highest Soviet official is orthodoxy, the will of any who happens not to have drunk too deeply at the Soviet wells of propaganda is clouded with fear. We therefore cannot rule out the possibility that the Soviet Government may mistakenly feel free to proceed so far towards a showdown with us as to use overt force to install Communist governments in western Europe, and hence the possibility that without its deliberately choosing war, war there may be.

But on balance, accepting Mr. Stimson's assumption [3] that some among the Russian leaders have a respect for facts, we may provisionally conclude that the Soviet Union is not prepared for war now and is not seeking the ultimate showdown. The hallmark of the "revolutionary situation" which precedes the act of revolution is the collapse of the governing power. This "collapse" is what the Soviet Government is evidently aiming to produce in Europe now through its program of planned social and economic disintegration. Against that program we set our program of

[3] "The Challenge to Americans." *Foreign Affairs*, October 1947.

planned reconstruction. We know that it involves risks. We know that the execution of it will tax our wisdom, our patience and our pocketbooks. We undertake it because we must. We can draw encouragement for the outcome, spiritual as well as material, from the knowledge that Europe wants what we can give and Soviet Russia cannot—material help—and that with it we offer what Soviet Russia will not—political freedom.

Part II

TO STRENGTHEN U.N.

1.

We have learnt that the people of Europe must have bread in their stomachs before they can digest political ideas. We are preparing to help with bread now for the meals immediately ahead, and studying a correlated program of help and self-help which will make it possible for them in the long run to earn again their own bread. We are heartened to proceed with our share in this plan by the fact that as soon as it began to take shape the situation in Europe began to be transformed. Suddenly it became apparent that confidence and resourcefulness are contagious, that with even a little encouragement time would work for those who believe that Europe's civilization is worth saving and can be saved instead of for those who believe that it must and can be destroyed. There was, in a word, a rebirth of hope—hope in Europe, and hope in America.

To the rulers of Soviet Russia this return of hope to Europe was infuriating. What could they do to prevent its return to the world as a whole? In many directions they sensed that their long-term plans for spreading chaos as a breeding ground for Communism had encountered a check. In the United Nations their delegates found themselves at an intolerable disadvantage—the novel disadvantage which confronts the beneficiaries of a police-state when, venturing abroad, they are subjected to the "impertinences" (a favorite word with Mr. Vishinsky) of free discussion, orderly argument, factual rebuttal, legalized disagreement and even (as Hitler would have put it) "unheard-of downright opposition."

Soviet apprehensions of the hazards of the world forum had been present from the start—and earlier than the start—of the United Nations. But only in the course of 1947 did the tactics of the Soviet representatives reveal fully that the same sense of insecurity which had dominated Soviet policy in Europe was driving them to dig a trench between themselves and most other members of the United Nations.

By the time the General Assembly of the United Nations met in September 1947 the atmosphere was plainly that of a crisis. As the sessions continued the crisis deepened. The cause of this crisis in the United Nations was generally assumed to be the long and progressive deterioration in the relations of the United States and the Soviet Union. Are we not justified, without being too smug, in putting the case the other way around? Is it not historically and psychologically more correct to say that it was Soviet policy, as given concrete application in the United Nations, which produced the crisis; and that this in turn aggravated Soviet-American friction to the point where it was mistaken for the cause instead of being recognized as a manifestation of the deeper conflict?

The fact of growing Soviet-American tension is not in dispute. Elmo Roper's public opinion polls taken in July 1946 and July 1947 reveal it mathematically on the American side; and if the decibel system of measurement could be applied to the crackle of paper and spurt of ink as *Pravda* and *Izvestia* editors prepare their daily pieces, and to the reverberations of Mr. Vishinsky's oratory through the air-conditioned assembly chamber at Flushing Meadows, it doubtless would confirm the belief that an even profounder irritation has developed in Soviet Russia. Mr. Roper disclosed that in July 1946 the number of Americans who looked on Russia as a peace-loving nation, willing to fight only in self-defense, was about the same as the number who thought of her as aggressive, willing to start a war to get something she wanted. One year later, in July 1947, the percentage of those questioned that thought of Russia as peace-loving had shrunk from 38.6 to 12.3, and the percentage that thought of her as aggressive had leapt up from 37.8 to 65.5.[4] The deterioration in Soviet-American relations must then be accepted as an unhappy fact. What principally caused it, and why did it occur so abruptly?

The Soviet effort to build a puppet wall around the vast Russian periphery would hardly have been enough, in and of itself, to bring American resent-

[4] *New York Herald Tribune*, October 16, 1947.

ment against the Soviet Government so rapidly to such
a pitch. Rather, most Americans would have continued to regard Soviet actions in Eastern Europe—as
many experts and fairminded editorial writers at first
had done—as unfortunate and uncalled-for but not
unnatural carryovers of the ingrained suspicion toward
the West which had developed in Russia, not without
some reason, from 1918 on.

Nor would earlier Soviet manoeuvres on specific
issues before the Security Council have been sufficient,
without apparent confirmation in the deeper wells of
long-range Soviet policy, to create anything more
serious in the average American mind than a sort of
baffled annoyance. In the Iranian affair, the Soviet dele-
gate had finally bowed to the insistence of his
colleagues that, in accordance with Soviet promises
and Iranian demands, Soviet troops be withdrawn
from northern Iran; and in the Albanian affair,
though he fought to exonerate Albania from the
charge of mining the Corfu Channel and causing the
death of British seamen, he was willing, in the end,
to abstain from vetoing the reference of the dispute to
the World Court, thereby saving the Security Council
from entire frustration. Indeed, until the summer of
1947 there were reasons to argue that, despite the harsh
things often said during the debates in the Security
Council, that organ of the United Nations was not to
be written off as invariably and permanently incapaci-
tated from action by the Soviet use of the veto.

In the realm of ideology, similarly, there is no reason to suppose that the spiritual conflict between democracy and Communism would have determined in practice the actions of our Government in matters affecting the Soviet Government to any greater extent during the postwar period than had been the case before the war. Rather the contrary. The abolition of the Comintern in 1943 had been accepted abroad as a conciliatory move on Moscow's part, and thenceforward expression of the American antipathy for Communism was generally restricted (outside certain important religious and economic groups and their newspaper and Congressional spokesmen) to attacks on "Reds" in the United States. Indicative of the mixed feelings about Soviet Russia prevailing during the war was the character in newspaper cartoons labelled, not altogether disrespectfully, "Uncle Joe." Frequently he was depicted against a hedge of bayonets, but with a rather jovial smile on his face. We may therefore presume (supported also by past American attitudes toward Fascism and Nazism) that the ideological pull between the Communist and democratic loadstones would have had to materialize in a conflict of material interests before it carried the American people beyond the point of reprobating Communism morally and criticizing it verbally. It would hardly have been powerful enough to destroy in two years the admiration which had been felt by most Americans for the embattled Russian people at Moscow and Stalingrad,

the desire to help them which had led to the shipment
of more than 11 billion dollars' worth of American
supplies to the Soviet Union during the war, and the
willingness to go into partnership with them on a
long-term live-and-let-live basis which had been signi-
fied by the Senate's 89-to-2 vote to accept the United
Nations Charter.

Really decisive, I believe, was the Soviet refusal to
assist the United Nations in strengthening and filling
out the mechanism which would make the Security
Council and its various organs into a reliable and
ready instrument against aggression. Achievement of
that goal had been fixed in American minds by President Roosevelt and Secretary Hull as the only reward
which would justify the sacrifices and sufferings of
the war. This does not mean that Americans mini-
mized the other functions of the United Nations. They
looked to the General Assembly to provide useful opportunities for all countries, small and big, to discuss
their problems freely and to mobilize the world's public opinion behind solutions which commended themselves to its conscience. They hoped that the work of
the various economic, health, educational and other
agencies would lessen the underlying causes of war.
They could see a valuable place for the International
Court in helping settle certain types of national dis-
agreements. But the first, chief and continuing American interest was whether the Security Council could
organize increasing security against an armed attack

by one nation on another. It seems plain that in 1947 they lost hope that the Security Council could do this; and they laid responsibility for the failure on Soviet Russia.

In accepting the Charter in the summer of 1945 the American people had sacrificed some of their dearest shibboleths of national sovereignty. And in the ensuing two years they gave strong indications that if the other Great Powers were willing to move forward toward a still more comprehensive and clear-cut system of security the Administration would be free to move forward with them.

This new attitude was demonstrated most strikingly, perhaps, in the popular support given to the Administration's position with regard to atomic energy. The United States proposed to forego using the terrible new engines of atomic destruction which it had mainly developed and which it alone at the moment possessed, provided only a method could be found to make sure that no other nation would develop and use them. For this purpose it suggested a method of control which most of the other nations found practicable and fair; and it offered (and demanded) that the veto should not apply to the punishment of infringements. The American public, through Congress and the press, endorsed this proposal.

Another instance of the public's concern for the essentials of security and peace, quite apart from the interest it took in the Security Council's antics as a sort of sporting event, was the widespread approval given the treaty negotiated by the United States and the other American Republics at Rio de Janeiro early in September 1947. This treaty committed its signatories to act against aggression in the Western Hemisphere, not by unanimity, as provided in the Charter, but by a two-thirds vote. It revealed how thoroughly the American public and Congress (represented at Rio by Senators Vandenberg and Connally and Representative Bloom) had determined to commit themselves to positive actions to establish security and maintain peace.

The fact is that American opinion would have repudiated an American policy which did not aim to strengthen and support the Charter in positive terms. Specifically, it expected the prompt adoption of a plan for the control of atomic energy, a project for the limitation of armaments and an agreement which implemented the Charter enforcement procedure by providing the international forces needed to deal with an act of aggression on the spot. When nothing of the sort occurred, people looked to see who was holding back, and when enough time had passed to make clear that the attitude of Mr. Molotov, Mr. Vishinsky and Mr. Gromyko must represent a deliberate decision on the part of the Soviet Government, the effect on American popular feeling towards the Soviet Union was disastrous.

The effect on our Government policy could not but

be profound also. It sometimes is forgotten how radi-
cally our acceptance of the Charter altered the basis on
which we conduct our foreign relations. Our position
toward other nations is no longer determined pri-
marily by propinquity or distance, or by economic,
cultural, religious or ideological affinity or repulsion.
These things continue to count. But when the time
comes for our Government to cast up its accounts
with another nation and adopt a positive attitude toward it, the fact that the United States is a member of
the United Nations introduces a new determinant
which may be decisive: Is that nation fulfilling its
promise to work toward peace and security under the
Charter? The President and the Secretary of State
must often have asked themselves this question about
the Soviet Union in the past year; and as time passed
without any progress being made toward implement-
ing the practical procedures of the United Nations for
maintaining peace they must have come to feel that at
least in this particular the answer could hardly fail to
be: It is not.

2.

Already at Yalta it was seen that the Soviet Union
wished to restrict the positive functions of the United
Nations in maintaining peace. But the real evidence

came at San Francisco the evening of June 1, 1945,
when there fell a Soviet bombshell in the form of a
demand that the veto be applicable at the very start
of the Security Council procedure for settling disputes.
On instructions from Moscow, Mr. Gromyko demanded that the Security Council should be deprived
of the right even to discuss and consider a complaint
from an aggrieved or threatened state without the
unanimous agreement of all the five permanent members. This radical modification of the Yalta under-
standing was rejected by Secretary of State Stettinius.
He won his point, however, only after making a blunt
statement to Marshal Stalin (through Harry Hopkins,
who happened to be in Moscow at the moment) that
continued insistence by the Soviet on its interpretation
would disrupt the conference.

The American delegation at San Francisco tried
further to turn the tide against broadening the use
of the veto by inserting into a joint interpretative statement issued by the "Big Five" on June 8 a sentence to
the effect that they were not expected to "use their
'veto' power willfully to obstruct the operation of the
Council." Like their British and French colleagues,
the American delegates (including Senators of both
parties) felt that the Great Powers which were to bear
the major responsibility for giving effect to any Security Council decision, and especially, of course, one
involving military operations, must have the veto as
protection against possible irresponsible action by a ma-

jority of the smaller states. And this position can be defended on democratic grounds as well as by the argument of pure expediency. However, the American conception of the veto was that it would be used for major purposes alone; and the American delegation hoped that the sentence quoted above, accepted by the Soviet Union along with the other Great Powers, would lessen the likelihood of the veto's being used to obtain tactical advantages or block ordinary decisions of the Council majority.

In practice, however, the veto has plainly not been used in accordance with that interpretation. By the time the General Assembly met in September 1947, the Soviet Union had resorted to the veto in the Security Council 18 times;[5] and it has used it since on such theoretically formal questions as the admission of additional members to the United Nations. The result is that, whether by "willful" design or not, the operation of the Security Council is certainly "obstructed."

Before the Security Council could perform its prime duty of organizing security it had to perfect in practice the machinery created by the Charter and in addition provide those other parts of the mechanism for which the Charter simply supplied specifications. As nations brought it complaints, it had to learn how to keep the procedure for the peaceful settlement of dis-

---

[5] The veto had also been used once by the Soviet Union and France together, and once by France alone.

putes in operation through graduated stages of speed
and pressure. In preparation for carrying out what
would be the final phase in any positive action required under the Charter, it had to organize the international forces needed to defeat aggression and
restore peace and security. Simultaneously, its subsidi-
ary commissions had to devise an equitable and effective method of controlling atomic energy and a
practicable scheme of progressive disarmament.

In these fundamental endeavors the Security Council and its organs have found themselves hamstrung
by the necessity of Great Power unanimity. By the
autumn of 1947 the Council's most routine activities
had become stalemated; and with the fundamental
problem of organizing security it and its commissions
were wrestling in vain.

3.

Now in signing the Charter, nations assumed general
as well as specific obligations. In the very first article
they asserted their Purposes: to maintain peace and
security; to take effective collective measures for the
prevention and removal of threats to the peace; and
to suppress acts of aggression. In support of these Purposes, they bound themselves to observe certain Principles. They agreed to fulfill in good faith their under-

takings under the Charter; to settle their disputes by peaceful means; not to threaten or use force against another state except in fulfillment of the Purposes of the Charter; and to give the United Nations every assistance in collective actions undertaken by it in accordance with the Charter.

These obligations are expressed, of course, in general terms. But they are not for that reason the less binding. Nor do they represent simply perfunctory (or even sincere) expressions of benevolent intent; those were reserved for the Preamble. No, these are not mere "whereas" preliminaries, but an integral part of the Charter, as binding on all members as any specific clause.

Through 1947 the strong nations became increasingly restless that obligations existed without adequate means having been provided for carrying them into effect. The small nations became more and more frightened at the delays of the powerful nations in agreeing among themselves how to execute the responsibilities which they had demanded and assumed. Large and small, most of the members of the United Nations began looking for means to put the organization in a position to carry out its Purposes and Principles.

The nations which opposed the veto most strongly at San Francisco still demanded, of course, that it be rescinded. But this could be done only by a change in the Charter; and changes in the Charter are subject to veto. The same obstacle confronted the less drastic and eminently reasonable proposal of ex-Secretary Stimson and others that, as a first step in invigorating the United Nations, the veto be restricted to measures requiring the use of armed force, thus freeing the procedure for the peaceful settlement of disputes from being blocked by one Power. There has been no sign that the Soviet Union would accept this restriction of its veto prerogative.

Secretary Marshall in September 1947 invited the General Assembly to undertake responsibility for some of the things which the Security Council had shown it could not do. To meet the difficulty that the Assembly comes together in regular session only once annually, he proposed that it set up an Interim Committee to function between sessions. However, the Assembly is also handicapped by the fact that its functions are strictly limited; and so will be the Interim Committee, since even if no specific bounds had been set to its powers it can exercise none which its parent does not have. The Assembly can discuss any question within the scope of the Charter (one of the toughest fights of the American delegation at San Francisco was to establish this right); it can (as in the Palestine case) set up an investigating body; and it can make recommendations, but only regarding a matter which is not before the Security Council. This last prohibition might tie the hands of the Interim Committee at the very start of a world crisis; for any member could bring the dispute before the Security Council and thereby automatically prevent the Assembly or its committee from making any recommendations regarding it. True, the Security Council can relinquish consideration of a question by a simple procedural vote of 7 of the 11 members (*e.g.* the veto of the permanent members does not apply); but while it had a proposal to do this under discussion the Interim Committee would be helpless and the aggressor nation might carry its aggression to a successful conclusion. Furthermore, even if the jurisdictional question were cleared up, the right of the Interim Committee to make a recommendation might be challenged and its recommendation disregarded. Soviet Russia's attitude toward the whole idea of an Interim Committee, which she considers contrary to the letter and spirit of the Charter, forecasts that she would resist or at least boycott any activities it might undertake (as she has announced her intention of boycotting the Greek border commission and the Korean election commission). There remains, of course, the force of world opinion which might be aroused by a full discussion in the Interim Committee. This force is far from negligible; but viewed realistically it does not seem likely by itself to alter a fundamental Soviet position once it has been adopted and announced by Moscow.

4.

This does not mean, however, that no effective step is possible within the framework of the United Nations. There is nothing in either the letter or spirit of the Charter which forbids members from agreeing among themselves, in more explicit terms than those used in the Charter, to carry out the organization's Principles and Purposes by more efficient methods than those which the Charter itself provides. Indeed, Article 51 of the Charter expressly reserves to members the inherent right of individual or collective self-defense in the event of armed attack against a member. In making preparations to exercise this right, members would not be planning anything which they had said they would not do; they would be planning only what they had said they might have to do, and arranging to do it in spite of difficulties and dangers which they had hoped would not arise.

The United States Government has announced its willingness to relinquish the right to veto collective action against a nation violating the projected atomic energy controls. It agreed at Rio on September 2, 1947, that the collective measures against aggression described in the Act of Chapultepec shall be put into effect by a two-thirds vote of the contracting parties. Is it now willing to move further along this course and modify its right to veto collective action against a member of the United Nations which makes an armed attack against another member?

Let us at this point grasp a nettle and calculate opposing risks. If we modify or abandon our veto power is there a risk that the majority of the middle-sized and small nations will involve us in war? The answer is that the majority of the smaller nations are desperately anxious to avoid being caught in a war. In the reality of practical politics, the risk is not that they will want to join in making war, even as our allies, but that they will hold back too long from a fateful decision which has become evidently necessary. And what about the converse, the possibility that the majority of the middle-sized and smaller nations will join with our potential enemies and make war against us? The answer is that if the world situation deteriorates so far, we face a war in any event, and no formal votes will either hasten or hinder it. Could we, for example, conceive that the Soviet rulers would be deterred by a legalism if they felt that, regardless of the votes of smaller states, they controlled a preponderance of physical power in the world?

If the President and Secretary of State find these answers to possible objections valid, they might propose that a group of United Nations members enter into a brief supplementary agreement—a sort of protocol, or "optional clause," open to all—binding themselves to carry out the Charter obligation to resist armed attack. This agreement would be worded so as to come into operation: 1, if two-thirds of the signatories decided that collective action was called for under the Charter; and 2, if the Security Council failed to act.

The suggested two-thirds majority not only is the same as that required under the Rio treaty for hemispheric action; it is the same as that which will govern decisions taken in the Interim Committee of the General Assembly. Another precedent of a different sort is found in an event which occurred in February 1946. Seven members of the Security Council voted to permit Britain and France to enter into direct negotiations with Syria and Lebanon for the withdrawal from those countries of British and French troops. Russia vetoed the proposal. But Britain and France nevertheless complied with the will of the majority of their colleagues.

Provision would have to be made in the protocol to bridge the present gap in the enforcement procedure of the United Nations. The Charter states that member nations should put armed forces at the disposal of the Security Council to enable it to carry out its decisions, but thus far the Military Staff Committee has been unable to fix the national quotas. These contributions would have to be agreed upon among the parties to the protocol at the time of signing.

The existence of the protocol might spur the United Nations to fill out its enforcement procedure and qualify the use of the veto. In this way, the protocol might in time become superfluous. Meanwhile, it would obviate efforts to amend the Charter in order to permit something less than unanimity in commencing sanctions in certain circumstances—for instance, violation of the atomic controls or armed attack on a member.

It will be recalled that an attempt was made in 1924 to strengthen the League of Nations through the so-called Geneva Protocol, which was designed to link up the League's disarmament program with a system for the compulsory settlement of disputes and joint action against aggression. The Geneva Protocol marked the turning point in the destinies of the League. Had it been adopted, the course of world events in the next decade might have been very different. But the plan fell through, largely because the British Government, which under Ramsay MacDonald had been favorable, decided after Mr. Baldwin's advent to power not to increase its direct commitment to act against aggression. A factor in this decision was Canada's notification to the Mother Country that it would not be entangled in Europe's quarrels. The situation is quite different today. The British Dominions no longer put their hope and trust for peace in attempts to remain aloof from foreign commitments; indeed, at San Francisco they led the campaign for an enforcement procedure free of the veto.

The proposal here made does not conflict with the Interim Committee of the General Assembly; on the contrary, it can be construed as a further move in the same direction, and, indeed, has been so described by

Senator Vandenberg.[6] A general current of feeling favorable to a modification of the veto seems to have set in, some of it arising in unexpected quarters—for example, with Senator Taft. Nobody would pretend, of course, that the mere adoption of the suggested supplementary protocol would automatically solve all the problems now frozen by the veto. It nevertheless might make the solution of some of them easier. A compromise between the rival concepts for controlling atomic energy might be found more readily if the bomb were already at the disposal of an international force actually in being. The limits within which armaments could be reduced would become clearer once national quotas for that force had been fixed. Covert aggression in the form of propaganda, threats, infiltration of agents and fifth-column activities would not be eliminated; neither the Charter as it now stands nor any other formula so far suggested can do that. But the terror and effectiveness of indirect aggression might be diminished if menaced governments could have confidence that it was not likely to be the precursor of direct aggression, or that if an armed attack should come they would not have to resist it alone.

[6] Letter to the author, published with Senator Vandenberg's authorization by T. J. Hamilton in *The New York Times,* September 6, 1947.

5.

For certain members of the United Nations to agree to carry out the Purposes and Principles of the United Nations in case the mechanism of the United Nations does not function, and until it does, could not properly be considered an unfriendly act by any member of the United Nations. If a member felt it was being discriminated against, it could at once attain equality by signing too. The fact must nevertheless be faced that any effort to extricate the United Nations enforcement provisions from the vise of the overworked veto would almost certainly be taken in Moscow as directed against the Soviet Union.

This might have both unfortunate and fortunate consequences. We would regret to give Soviet Russia added reason to feel that we are unfriendly to her; for though we hate dictatorship and oppose Communism, we have not been without hope of finding means of living alongside the Communist dictatorship in conditions of peace and even, in time, of mutual trust. Nevertheless, we do desire to impress upon the Soviet Union's leaders with all possible seriousness that the preponderant forces of the world are likely to be thrown instantly and decisively into the scale against aggression, and that Russia no more than any other nation in the world can count on being immune from the results of such collective action.

The Soviet Union has already revealed the extent of her present suspicion of the democratic nations. For them to say frankly just what they would do in case of aggression by her or one of her satellites could hardly increase her suspicions by much. Moreover, if the assertions of the men in the Kremlin that they do not seek the ultimate showdown of war now are sincere (as many circumstances described earlier would indicate), they may be glad to be spared ambiguities in the policy of other nations which might land them, unawares, in a war they had not planned.

No one could tell thirty years ago what would be the final form and spirit of the new Communist entity which had just sprung forth from the corpses of the Russian past, real and figurative. No one can tell today. At that time, however, it at least seemed to the good that the crust of the old tyranny had been broken and that the unknown but gifted Russian masses, so long clamped down beneath it, were about to have a chance to assert their needs and claim their rights. The revolution had appalling aspects, and the possible courses of development included some that were terrifying. But other revolutions undertaken by populations long and greatly oppressed had had appalling aspects, and in the end had evolved into régimes with which other nations had been able to live in amity.

There was no illusion in the West that the Russian

revolution, by merely breaking the Tsarist chains, had automatically released the Russian people to freedom, plenty and peace. After smothering for many centuries in serfdom, they could not be expected to rise up instantly clothed with all the aptitudes for tolerant self-government developed by other nations through slow years of education and conscious effort. There nevertheless seemed no inexorable reason to despair that some day they would be able to create a modern civilized state, capable not merely of serving their own needs but also of exercising a mighty influence for universal peace and progress.

We shall not entirely despair today. But having faced and dealt with the problem of Nazi Germany we know more than we did before about the nature of dictatorships—in particular, more about their fallibilities and the mistakes they can make. We have seen the folly of asserting that such-and-such a nation "is in no condition to fight"; we also know that dictators can and do commit that folly. Hitler thought that Chamberlain's Britain could not resist him and that Britain knew she could not; he therefore felt certain she would make no attempt to do so. He dismissed respectful estimates of the American war potential with a contemptuous *"Das Alles ist Bluff."* Stalin thought that Hitler's Germany could not risk war on two fronts.

A military dictatorship's pride, its ability to mold its own public opinion and (for all the brains and intensive work which go into the making of its poli-

cies) its essential ignorance about how free peoples
think and act—these combine to create a constant risk
of war in the world. The Soviet oligarchy may well be
laboring today under the mistaken belief that the British, struggling back to their feet after five grueling
years of war and two disillusioning years of peace, will
not dare to stand, or will be too weak to stand, where
they stood before. Or it may suppose that the American
people, soon to be caught (so runs the rubric) in a
tailspin of economic collapse and social disintegration,
will not be ready, able and willing to take up again,
if they must, the unfinished fight of a generation ago,
still apparently unfinished after another world war,
for the right of peoples everywhere to self-government,
security and peace.

The risks inherent in permitting such grave miscon-
ceptions as these to continue might be diminished by
strengthening the United Nations by adopting the
proposed protocol. We must calculate them anxiously
against the risks which strong action would itself
create. One advantage of the protocol is that it provides
an alternative to force and as such would gain time;
this may indeed be its chief attraction, if there is virtue
in the theory that even though the Soviet régime may
not "mellow" with age (a term made controversial by
Mr. X in his *Foreign Affairs* article), it may at least
lose through long frustration its hope of acquiring
control of the world by force. The written provisions
of the Charter, as has been pointed out by Mr. St.

Laurent, the Canadian Minister of External Affairs, are not a ceiling over the responsibilities of member states, but a floor under them. The action here suggested would be in harmony with that statement. The aim is not to sacrifice the United Nations to independent action, but to strengthen and save it; not to signalize the end of the hopes the world knew in 1945, but to reassert them and give them new assurance; not to prepare for war, but to preserve peace.

CONCLUSION

"The climax of all battles," said Churchill, "is anxious." Today we are in the crisis of two struggles which are not military but nevertheless may be as decisive for the future of the world as any of the great battles of history. They are the struggles to help Europe save herself and to help strengthen the United Nations and give it time to prove itself. The costs and risks we assume in entering these two struggles are recognizably great, and will be greater.

But the resources we bring to the struggle are great also. And today there are appearing alongside us, in Europe and in the councils of the United Nations, instinctive forces that well up from the deep being of all mankind and that will not be downed by any oppression or threat. Bullying always provokes resentment, brutal force always creates resistance and revolt. The tide of history still runs in the direction of freedom all through the world.

History has given us, what it rarely does, a second chance; and by an almost unanimous decision of the Senate we have this time chosen to accept the challenge which we rejected in 1920. We have decided to work toward a settlement of the world's disputes in terms of the Purposes and Principles of the United Nations Charter. By our acceptance of the enforcement provisions of the Charter, too, we have shown this time that we know that the powers of peace are not made effective by a mere declaration of good intentions. We now have to decide, calculating the opposing risks carefully and calmly, whether, if those enforcement provisions cannot be given effect unanimously, we should join with other likeminded nations in undertaking to give them effect to the fullest extent that lies within our joint and collective powers.

If we are sufficiently convinced that we have been steering the right course, and accept gladly its hazards, we may still, with the tide of mankind's stubborn love of freedom flowing strongly with us, bring the ship of peace into port.